It's OK, Jesus Loves You Anyway!

It's OK, Jesus Loves You Anyway!

Glenn Goree

Foreword by
Demetrius Donseroux

RESOURCE *Publications* · Eugene, Oregon

IT'S OK, JESUS LOVES YOU ANYWAY!

Copyright © 2015 Glenn Goree. All rights reserved. Except for brief quotations in critical publications or reviews, no part of this book may be reproduced in any manner without prior written permission from the publisher. Write: Permissions. Wipf and Stock Publishers, 199 W. 8th Ave., Suite 3, Eugene, OR 97401.

Resource Publications
An Imprint of Wipf and Stock Publishers
199 W. 8th Ave., Suite 3
Eugene, OR 97401

www.wipfandstock.com

ISBN 13: 978-1-4982-1919-8

Manufactured in the U.S.A.   01/23/2015

This book is dedicated to our mother Neva Goree. She taught us the deeper meanings of right and wrong and is the corner stone and foundation of our family.

Contents

Foreword by Demetrius Donseroux | ix

    Introduction | 1
1. Divided Heart | 3
2. Who Deserves Anger's Flame? | 4
3. Hunger's Cure | 5
4. Doubt's Darkness | 6
5. Alone? | 7
6. Never Satisfied | 8
7. Internment | 9
8. A Flag to be Unfurled | 10
9. Lost in Darkness | 11
10. The Beginning of Wisdom | 12
11. The Beginning of Understanding | 13
12. Where Have I Seen These Eyes Before? | 14
13. Fruit on a Vine | 15
14. Pride Blinds | 16
15. Beyond Self | 17
16. In the Grip of Vice | 18
17. God's Love | 19
18. How I live | 20
19. Crimson Stain | 21
20. What is Sin? | 23
21. Humility | 24
22. Choices | 25
23. Salvation | 26
24. Jesus Loves You Anyway | 27

Foreword

GLENN AND I MET during a time of great transition in my life. I was pursuing my doctorate degree and I was starting a counseling practice. I wanted my practice to be centrally located in an environment where people would feel comfortable sharing their inner narratives. Moreover, I wanted my practice to focus on Christian values like love, peace, and joy. I am convinced that the Holy Spirit led me to Glenn. He is the clinical director of a faith-based counseling center. Glenn and I quickly developed a beneficial relationship; one based on mutual respect and admiration for the diversity of people who desire to experience a life free of guilt and shame built on past and present bad decisions.

Since our first encounter, Glenn and I have regularly met and discussed the need for dynamic tools that can help people live the abundant life that Jesus described in John 10:10. Glenn has taken a giant leap forward with this collection of poetry. *"It's OK, Jesus loves you anyway"* provided me with comfort and reassurances despite my inability to live a sinless life. The poems reinforced the simple but important fact that Jesus is ready, willing, and able to forgive my trespasses. Furthermore, the poems highlight God's unfathomable love for me. I am convinced that any person who desires to experience God's love via the written word, will receive comfort and assurances as they read through the poems in this book. Glenn has done a masterful job of explaining the spirit of the biblical narrative of Romans 7:7-24. I pray that all who read these poems, Christian or not, will have their hearts opened by the Holy Spirit and experience the full love of Jesus.

Shalom,

Demetrius Donseroux, LPC, Ph.D.
Adjunct Professor of Counseling

Introduction

"It's OK, Jesus loves you anyway." In my thirty-year counseling career, I've repeated this sentence over and over to my clients. No matter the counseling setting, people need this exoneration because they usually have one common complaint—a belief they've committed the unpardonable sin, and are overwhelmed by guilt.

Clients experience guilt at three levels. First, they know intellectually that Jesus has forgiven them of their sins because of what they've read in the Bible. But next, there are two emotional levels they have to fight through in order to accept God's grace. People should learn to receive God's forgiveness, and then they need to forgive themselves. This last level is the most difficult one for them to accept.

There is one universal reason some clients refuse to accept self-forgiveness. These burdened souls believe if they were really *good* Christians, they wouldn't have been tempted in the first place! Guilt assaults their consciences under two misconceptions—a belief of committing an unforgivable sin, and guilt for succumbing to temptation. To overcome this struggle between the flesh and the spirit, these clients need to internalize the words of the Apostle Paul found in the book of Romans 7:14—8:2.

> "For we know that the law is spiritual, but I am of the flesh, sold under sin. For I do not understand my own actions. For I do not do what I want, but I do the very thing I hate. Now if I do what I do not want, I agree with the law, that it is good. So now it is no longer I who do it, but sin that dwells within me. For I know that nothing good dwells in me, that is, in my flesh. For I have the desire to do what is right, but not the ability to carry it out. For I do not do the good I want, but the evil I do not want is what I keep on doing. Now if I do what I do not want, it is no longer I who do it, but sin that dwells within me.
>
> "So I find it to be a law that when I want to do right, evil lies close at hand. For I delight in the law of God, in my inner being, but I see in my members another law waging war against the law of my mind and making me captive to the law of sin that dwells in my members. Wretched man that I am! Who will deliver me from this body of death? Thanks be to God through Jesus Christ our LORD! So then, I myself serve the law of God with my mind, but with my flesh I serve the law of sin and death.

Introduction

> "There is therefore now no condemnation for those who are in Christ Jesus. For the law of the Spirit of life has set you free in Christ Jesus from the law of sin and death." (ESV)

What we learn here from Paul is that temptation comes from the constant spiritual battle between the spirit and the flesh. All people experience this struggle, without exception, except Jesus Christ. In this conflict, sometimes the spirit wins, and sometimes the flesh is victorious—a reality of life. Paul concluded his teachings on this struggle as stated in the above quotation of Rom 8:1–2. Jesus Christ does forgive and he sets us free from guilt and shame.

Here are several questions I'd like to ask. Are you experiencing a struggle between the flesh and spirit over alcohol or drug addiction? It's OK, Jesus loves you anyway. Is pornography waging a war between your eyes and your will? It's OK, Jesus loves you anyway. Are you experiencing the seven year itch? It's OK, Jesus loves you anyway.

No matter what form or type of struggle you're experiencing, Jesus will always love you. He's also there because of His desire to help you win. And if you lose, He will be there to pick up the pieces of your life.

This book of twenty-four poems is a symphony of thoughts about what Paul wrote in Romans. The poems were inspired by my thirty years of listening to clients' pain produced by their guilt, and my feelings of helplessness in trying to communicate that through Jesus they were set free. The thoughts expressed in these poems sort of poured out over a year or two, and were used to help Christians understand guilt was no longer a word they needed in their vocabulary.

I could have approached the topics in these poems from a theological or psychological perspective, but then in my opinion, it would have been just another book on guilt. My goal is to appeal to the intellect, heart, spirit, and soul of the reader. There is no way these poems can address guilt in the same manner Paul did. They are merely a commentary. So, no matter what your struggle may be, it's OK, Jesus loves you anyway.

1
Divided Heart

What is this battle frenzy in my heart?
Where did it divine its dividing art?

First, I want to, and then I don't.
Then I do, while crying, "I won't."

How does it position me skillfully so?
Why won't its fiendish grip let me go?

I see. I want. I devour.
Time matters not, nor the hour.

Yet, in sacred conscience, another I see.
There is a caring second side of me.

That which denies self, placing others first,
That part of me which offers a cup of water to quench a thirst.

Then, I witness the nature dark, pursuing wholeheartedly
That which feels good, but makes me cry despondently.

What will liberate me from this cursed torment?
How can I escape its torturous soul-crushing bent?

Perhaps if I'd been honest about my initial thought,
It would not have lured me into temptation's covert haunt.

If only I had listened to the former true voice calling,
Warning there is a deep, round, black caldron boiling,

I would not be embroiled in this mess I'm in,
And have to account for the consequences of my sin.

2
Who Deserves Anger's Flame?

Why do my legs hasten to forbidden, costly doors?
Why do my feet cross thresholds, dark and dim by the score?

Why do my arms hungrily and eagerly embrace?
Greedily succumbing to pleasure's beguiling disgrace?

What makes my hands burn like fire?
Why do they ravenously grasp with thoughtless passion's desire?

What makes me do what I swore only moments ago I would not?
What numbs sin's choice with less guiltless thought?

Surely my vision has not blindly betrayed,
Creating an illusion my fickle heart has made.

Can I not trust words, sweetly luring,
Promising a rose-colored future enduring?

If honest about my soul's predicament,
Perhaps it's me, not others to whom I should direct anger's bent?

Then, when I clearly see that I am alone,
It is I who should question my character's bone.

3
Hunger's Cure

What is this dank emptiness inside of me?
Why is it deep-set and as vast as the dark blue sea?

As far as the east is from the west,
Unlike God, its unforgiving pain is vast.

I long for a selfish hunger's cure,
As I can no longer tolerate it, nor endure.

Oh, vain wanton brief substitutes,
Do they not lure by jaded sight in fleshly lies as painted prostitutes?

The pit's deception and death is all they have to offer,
Momentary pleasure paid in full by fatality's lonely coffer.

After all has been tried and found sorely wanting,
What fills best this mortal life's lustful longing?

In none of this hapless world can it be found,
But it can only be discovered in the next, where souls abound.

And, as the majestic head sits alone,
Is there not found a God of love, on His eternal throne?

His manna of old no longer stills human hunger,
Nor any fleshly wants in dreams of slumber.

But He has new, cooling, refreshing water,
That quenches a parched thirst, so it lasts no longer,

And a new manna filling each soul's heartache,
So no more pain of sin will we partake.

4
Doubt's Darkness

Why is doubt's darkness so headstrong?
What makes my heart sing an ambivalent song?

I see, I want, but I'm in fear.
I question my heart's yearning, so I won't draw near.

This goal, this ambition, this vision in my mind,
I bid hasty retreat, time after time.

What is this hesitation that plagues me so?
Whose voice is this in me echoing, "No. No. No."?

Why is failure always in my forethought?
Why do I assume I'm lost before I start?

Who formed this nagging, castrating doubt?
What does it so loudly shout?

You can't. You won't. You will fail.
Your effort is of no avail.

5
Alone?

Like crawling in a burning desert, alone,
With plaguing thirst and hunger, not even a dry bone.

Like treading water in a vast ocean, alone,
The cold sea chilling warm flesh to the bone.

Like being surrounded on a crowded street, yet alone,
Each soul preoccupied with a world their own.

Like a night on a battle field, scared and alone,
Blinded by darkness and fear of not returning home.

Like sitting in a doctor's office, waiting alone,
Praying for a miracle over what is unknown.

Like madness raging behind prison bars, yet alone,
Sanity faintly cries out as loud as a broken megaphone.

Like growing old in an empty covenant, alone,
Because love turned to hate and neither party will atone.

Like standing next to a fresh grave, alone,
As a life companion sleeps quietly beneath earth and stone.

Are we truly alone?
Want can we say of this unknown?

No. We are never alone.
For there is one who is with us through every unknown.

Quietly He stands,
Offering His hands.

So why do we feel so alone?
Because we try to live outside His home.

6
Never Satisfied

Beyond the garden gate, Adam did explore,
Not alone, but with the One he did adore.

What lure, what enticement caught his eye?
Did he not know one step beyond meant he would die?

Having everything of his heart's desire,
Why let sin catch him in its quagmire?

Human nature did from the start
Have no bounds of satisfaction in his heart.

No matter what it wants, it will always want more,
For its selfish choice disregards a hellish future in store.

7
Internment

What is this prison I see?
Yet there are no walls surrounding me.
And who is that dark shadow, grinning triumphantly?

No keys to locked heavy iron doors,
No pacing in confined cells on cold cracked concrete floors.

Where are the guards that vigilantly watch every minute?
Where are the weapons to enforce my penance?

Despite these missing tools denying freedom,
Why do I feel confined, as though I live with them?

What has sentenced me to life without parole?
Can I not appeal to live in freedom's role?

I am imprisoned by the choices I've made,
One by one, drawing me to darkness's blinding shade.

Though conscience drew me to the far light,
Friend darkness beckoned with many alluring delights.

Oh, had I begun a different path.
Had I started as a tender child, only knowing my parents' wrath?

Is it too late to approach heaven's gate?
Can I right the wrongs, and start a righteous gait?

Oh, the will to do right is so powerfully strong,
But the intoxicating practice of the flesh plays another song.

Yes, I will. I know I must.
In my God, from this day on, I'll put my trust.

I'll be honest in my motives and thoughts.
Darkness will no longer blind me from what I ought.

8
A Flag to be Unfurled

Where have I seen you before?
Who fills the dark shadow outside my heart's door?
Whose face in my mind's eye demands more?

Is it good or evil I see,
As passions delight demands me more to be?

Sleepless nights exhaust me as I toss and turn.
Why is it for evil and not good I yearn?

Why do I hopelessly twist and pull,
As though on Satan's rope like a wild bull?

It could be easy to abandon sin,
Yet why does a voice in me say, "Give in."?

It seems I struggle between two worlds
As I try to decide which flag to unfurl.

9
Lost in Darkness?

Are we only Satan's animal fodder?
Can he deal with us in arrogant saunter?

Does he really have so much control?
Can he so easily exact a hapless soul?
Can we avoid paying him an eternal toll?

Here's the secret he fears the most—
An eternity in hell, he quivers like a ghost.

He may bid his sinister, appealing wares,
Tempting souls to taste damning snares.

But his offers have eternal consequences,
They collapse and fall like a broken fence.

When we realize his magic only works
If we partake in his dark tricks and quirks.

10
The Beginning of Wisdom

Five times or more the Bible recorded
Moses on his face before God, reported.

Trembling, he was never sure what to do,
Hence on his face he laid, removing his shoes.

To God this octogenarian did humbly plead,
"I'm only a sinful man of many a mortal need."

God's reply was, "'I am' will lead.
Army or cavalry you won't need."

Why would Moses embrace Mother Earth?
Why besmirch self for all he was worth?

Was not the soil soaked with Christ's blood?
Did not a cross from a tree start as a bud?

Moses knew on the soil he must always be.
For God from there led him to see.

11
The Beginning of Understanding

How does God reveal Himself to us?
A simple question causes such a fuss.

Can we witness Him in nature and science?
Yes, but we refuse to listen in proud defiance.

We ignore proof of Him every day,
Around us He is revealed in every way.

Sightless because we decline to see,
Refusing to appeal on bended knee.

What causes this spiritual disease?
Is it Satan who infects us with such ease?

No. The enemy is not Satan, or God, or even sin.
It's our arrogant hearts refusing to give in.

Insolence digs our hell-bound eternal graves,
Securing them for Satan in the way we behave.

Thank God for His mercy and grace.
In His heart we never lose our place.

12
Where have I seen these Eyes before?

I have stared deeply into Satan's eyes,
Is he not the master and father of all black lies?

With ease he casts his hypnotic malaise,
Ensnaring souls with his traitorous gaze.

At will he enters innocent, naïve hearts,
Virgin territory, where he plants his flag, then starts

Like a director leading his jaded play.
He knows every part and what to say.

Where have I seen him practicing his skill?
Orbs of deception reeling in his final kill.

Not in places men go in the dead of night,
Tickling senses craving momentary delight.

Each morn he's found in my heart's reflection,
As this is when I chose to ignore his endgame's deception.

13
Fruit on a Vine

I think two-in-one love has its seasons,
It matures and grows for its own reasons.

If we would but give it time,
We'd find it buds like ripe fruit on a vine.

Youth is far too hasty and insecure,
It demands blooms before buds mature.

Then, in haste and disappointment,
Wanting love before its sweet appointment,

Bud and vine are pulled up by their roots,
Then quickly crushed by brooding, disappointed boots.

Oh, if we would but only wait,
Like a patient gardener at his orchard gate,

We would taste love divine, at its peak
And see God's love in it that he did sneak.

14
Pride Blinds

If there is a God, I need him not.
Am I not the master of my lot?

Death came knocking on my arrogant door,
"Come with me," it said, to settle an eternal score.

Satan stood by, licking his lips
Salivating uncontrollably, hands on his hips.

It's so easy, like nabbing fish in a barrel,
Pride blinds from the straight and narrow.

Give me trinkets and baubles that flatter,
My ego soon swells beyond what really matters.

I, as a deluded master, become just another slave,
Ignoring that in this life, I was Satan's knave.

Oh LORD, pray help me always to see
You are more important than me,
Because I want to safely live with you eternally.

15
Beyond Self

Oh, what a barrier self can be!
Eclipsing my life's light in front of me.

Ruled by my selfish flesh and mind,
Sin passionately pursued in form and kind.

Senses tainted, darkened, enticing me so near,
All used by Satan. Please steer me clear!

Show me, teach me LORD, I plead,
I need to know how to make you my one and only need.

16

In the Grip of Vice

Why do I cling to vice so tenaciously?
When once in her seductive grip, she chokes the life out of me.

Why do I embrace her like a forbidden lover?
When I know her allure leads to death, as I too late discover.

What is this dark, forbidden hunger in me
That prefers wrong over right, which I choose not to see?

Why do I justify my unbridled passions
When I know they will rob me entry to eternal mansions?

What is this raging war between flesh and spirit,
Where the heart craves sin, yet the mind says, "Don't go near it."?

If vice and her lascivious brood are so wonderful,
Why are they pursued only when the moon is barely full?

If there is no danger that exists in what I feel,
Then after a brief moment, why do I feel like such a heel?

If succumbing to her beckoning call was right,
Then afterward, why do I feel it was an abuse of a natural appetite?

So, we learn that a hunger for vice and her sisters can never be satiated,
Because they leave us burdened with guilt, forever escalated.

And vice and her sinister coven, beyond rage and envy,
Will always exact a hidden price they collect as Satan's levy.

17
God's Love

What is it about God?
Why does He watch where my feet trod?

Why would He care?
Why would He dare?

What have I done to deserve His notice?
Is not my life fairly bogus?

Even when I try,
There's always within me a lie.

What could He possibly see in me?
Why give me redemption free?

Perhaps because I can't grasp His perfect love,
For I seek as a mortal man and not the Almighty high above.

18
How I live

What is this beyond mortal sight?
Who determines my eternal plight?

Is it God, or Jesus, or the Holy Spirit?
No. It's my life and how I chose to live it.

19
Crimson Stain

What is this crimson stain on my hands?
Why does it make such holy demands?

Why does it care what I do?
Why does it sting my heart when I say no to you?

Its stain can't be washed away!
It's refreshed by the evil I do and say.

Oh, crimson why do you burden me so?
Why in heaven's name won't you let me go?

Are you not troubled by the heartache you cause?
Why does your color shadow my mortal flaws?

At that question my soul's tear-drenched eyes,
Cast a pleading gaze toward the darkened skies.

There on a roughly hewn crossbeam of a tree,
Where not one, but two wounded crimson hands I see.

In each palm is driven a massive iron nail,
Tearing, ripping through His flesh to impale.

Then I hear a voice from of heavens say,
"It's for your soul this crimson is present each day.
Not to judge, but to save you from the earth's lost way.

Without these punctures in my Son's flesh,
Without His dying pain, no less,
There would be no payment for mortal's sin so enmeshed."

Crimson Stain

Then, I lay before my compassionate God,
Prostrate on earth's tear-drenched sod.

My face I place flat on the ground,
I dare not utter a human sound,

Until my heart can stand it no more,
As I realize His blood has evened sin's score.

Guilt-free, I declare and implore,
"Behold the Lamb who died once, with a plan in store,
Because of His crimson pain, I will live forevermore."

20
What is Sin?

What truthfully is sin?
Evil thoughts, or feelings, or where I've been?

Does transgression's birth belong to Adam and Eve?
Or is Satan, or me the one who deceives?

Shall we blame our sin on our Creator?
How opportune for our human nature!

Look at the motives in my heart.
Is darkness there where sin gets its start?

Is it lust or greed, envy or pride?
Or is this evil family caught in sin's tide?

Perhaps it's none of these at all,
When we see our souls embracing a fall.

One thing I know about sin for sure,
It has no power when in God I endure.

21
Humility

When this mortal frame
Returns to the earth from which it came,

A respectful posture will I seek,
Embracing Mother Earth as one meek.

When I was His thought in the womb,
Long before numbered days and the tomb,

Before Him I could show no deference.
But at death's door He deserves reverence.

How could any mortal stand,
When facing God who is in command?

It's by His grace and not our own,
His mercy in Christ's blood, no broken bone,

That in heaven and not with the devil,
He saved my soul for a path level.

22
Choices

Whose is this soft, gentle voice I hear,
Whispering anonymously in my mortal ear?

My heart is where it seems to be pouring from.
Why do I feel strangely uncomfortable when it's done?

Suggestion, observation, a nudge and innuendo,
Offer enticing options that urge me to go.

Subtle subversion is their master's terminal endgame,
Because he presents them as innocent, for the aroused flesh to entertain,

Oh, come on. These choices aren't really so bad!
Yet it's in these covert motives Satan's will is so naïvely clad.

They tenderly lead down slippery steps into his dark garden,
Deceiving me that my tomorrow will find hope's pardon.

"Oh LORD, I pray, help me to solely listen to you.
Teach me to hear your sweet voice in all that I do."

23
Salvation

Why does this feeble flesh of mine,
With sin's allure so easily entwine?

How does Satan know my flaws to excavate,
And discern how to entice, so I won't hesitate?

Before I detect sin's lie, with it I resonate,
Its hold so absorbing. Change is too late.

Then, deeper I tumble into outer darkness,
As I let go of Hope's salvation, I lose its brightness.

Just when I think all is gone astray,
A nail-scared hand reaches out to save the day.

I then hear a voice filled with compassion,
Stating, "A home for you in heaven He does fashion."

24
Jesus Loves You Anyway

It's OK,
Jesus loves you anyway.

It's all right,
Just continue the fight.

You'll be fine,
Jesus is with you all the time!

www.ingramcontent.com/pod-product-compliance
Lightning Source LLC
Chambersburg PA
CBHW061313040426
42444CB00010B/2627